FROM THE WOMB
OF GENTLENESS

FROM THE WOMB OF GENTLENESS

BINGZ HUANG

Yuanhui Chen, Melissa Blanchard

Huang Bingjie

Contents

Dedication   ix

Advanced Praise   1

HOW TO USE THIS BOOK

FOREWORD

                                                       8

HELLO

Poetry in a Bucket   10
The Womb of Gentleness   13

MY JOURNEY

A Sweet Bee 12 Hours From Me   16

How Gentle Can Gentleness Be?   18

Inside-Out   21

The Heart of Empathy 23

I Thank My Green Eyes 25

Holding Hands 27

Car Rides 31

My First and Only Fall 33

I Build Resilience With Gentleness 36

I Came From The Stars 39

My Kitchen Heaves a Sigh of Relief 42

Sketching Buses 45

Three Little Kittens 47

I'm a Hugger Mom 50

Everything is Fine 52

Will I Break? 55

Before The Twig Snaps 57

I Empower My Life With Gentleness 59

HEAL HUMANITY

If Life Is Just a Grand Illusion 62

Were You Called Down to Earth? 64

Come Home to You 66

Feel 68

QUICK REMINDERS

Stop Moving   72

Slow Down   73

Trust   74

Cry   75

Ocean's Wisdom   76

REBIRTH

I Used to Waffle   79

My Background Hum   82

Stay Bright   84

MORE ABOUT BINGZ AND YUANHUI

About the Author   88

About the Illustrator   90

Illustrated by Yuanhui Chen
Foreword by Melissa Blanchard
Edited by Aimée Gramblin

First Printing, 2020

I'm grateful to my angelic bee, shimmer fairy, nature witch, and all human and ethereal angels in my life.

Thank you for staying bright.

I love the way we shine. :)

Advanced Praise

"*From the Womb of Gentleness*, Bingz offers a poetic balance that zips, zings, and dances a heartful melody of honesty. Each poem has a flavor of love, depth, and transparency mixed with a whimsical, witty, playfulness. You will be enraptured with her joyfulness."
~ Carolyn M. Riker, LMHC,
Author of *My Dear, Love Hasn't Forgotten You.*

"I love this book! It is such a deep and refreshing read. Bingz echoes the words that many Mums have hidden and invites them to love themselves even more gently -- something we all need reminders for. This book makes a lovely gift from one gentle Mum to another!"
~ Sofie Hon, Founder of www.heartymums.com

"Bingz's poetry is to be savored. If you are in need of comfort in times of uncertainty, this book is for you. I treasure the words of wisdom sprinkled throughout. A gentle reminder of our magic and right to shine."
~ Dianna Lane, Intuitive Transformation Coach,
www.facebook.com/diannalanecoach

"Bingz's poetry transports you to this light, happy place filled with warmth and bright colors. They embody gentleness - in the truest sense of the word. I loved the poems with all my heart. This book is like the warm hug you didn't know you needed. :)"

 - Anangsha Alammyan, Author of *Stolen Reflections*, authoranangsha.com

"A delightful book that encourages us to take a gentle pause, journey within, and embrace our being through all of life's different moments."

 - Bernadette Chua, Managing Partner, www.positiveconsulting.sg

"As I began reading Bingz's poetry, I found myself smiling, tearing up. Her words and whimsical illustrations guided me to hold myself tenderly and playfully. I invite you to join me in re-reading this book again and again reminding us of the magical divine beings that we all are."

 -Viknesvari, Confidence Mentor, www.facebook.com/heArtflow.in

"This book is filled with tender love and gentleness, as it promises. It is an ideal gift for everyone who wants to feel loved. I am sure that your heart will explode with gentleness and humanitarian love once you soak your soul with this profound wisdom."

 - Darshak Rana, Top Writer in Poetry and Reading, darshakrana.medium.com

How to Use This Book

Dear Reader,

Aloha and thank you for being part of the experience of *From the Womb of Gentleness*.

From the Womb of Gentleness arose this collection of my poems and beautiful illustrations created by children's book illustrator, Yuanhui Chen.

If life feels extra intense for you right now, we gently encourage you to read this book like you are being invited to the warmth of the womb from the outside.

When you are ready to be open to the healing gift of Gentleness, we gently invite you to imagine stepping into this womb and allowing it to nurture you even more.

Some of the poems and illustrations here might help connect you with your unique life experiences, fears, thoughts, and feelings that want to unwind even more. Give yourself the time and space to process these.

Reconnect deeply with yourself.

This book is created to support you in being gentler with yourself and with your world. Thank you for being open to the magical medicine of Gentleness.

Aloha to you and forever,
Bingz and Yuanhui

Foreword

I am ecstatic to write this foreword, not only because I know Bingz Huang as a great friend, but also because I believe in the message of Gentleness Bingz inspires in the lives of those around her. I know about this magic as it continues to touch me every day.

I've been down many successful paths in my life, all of which need no specific mention as what I am proud of most is my passion for writing. I am currently a Top Writer in Poetry, Photography, Fiction, and Short Story on Medium, a writing and reading platform. I have also had the pleasure of co-editing two publications and my writing has been published in *Preferred Health Magazine*.

Above all, writing has led me down the path to incredible people like Bingz.

Have you ever met someone for the first time and left thinking, "Wow, what an incredible soul!"? You don't know much at that point, but you get a deep feeling, there is something magical about them. I felt that magic when I met Bingz on Medium.

As time went on, Bingz and I discovered that we connected on many levels, including mothering three children, a passion for the written word, and a love for music and dance. We are both empaths and sensitive souls. It's always an incredible feeling when you meet someone who feels as deeply as you do.

I remember when I first saw one of Bingz's dance videos! Her carefree and uninhibited presence made me smile, and her dancing gave me pure joy. Her long history with gentleness shines through in many ways.

I've had the honor to mentor Bingz in writing poetry. She was receptive, easy-going, and such a great listener. I'll never forget the energy we both felt and how we cried together during our call.

I imagine the gentle humans, *Gentleness Ambassadors* as Bingz named them, have felt exactly how I did when interacting with her. They have inspired her to write this wonderful book. These *Gentleness Ambassadors* have consistently expressed to Bingz how they appreciate talking about Gentleness versus Harshness.

As world events have become more chaotic over the years, Bingz feels a growing importance of bringing Gentleness in a way that speaks more to our hearts.

Immerse yourself in this book and feel Gentleness through various topics and situations in life. This book of poems is written in an open, honest, and freestyle form of poetry.

It embodies the many meanings of Gentleness from one of the most gentle people I know, Bingz.

Please use this book as a "womb" to cultivate Gentleness and I hope when you emerge, you will feel much more ready and willing to stay bright.

Feel Bingz Huang's magical heart in these poems as her peaceful nature brings out your Gentle soul.

Melissa Blanchard
Wife, Nurturing Mom of three children, Top writer, Co-editor, and Photographer

Take a few calming breaths, and enjoy the read. :)

Hello

What writing poetry means to me, and what this womb of Gentleness is about.

Poetry in a Bucket

my thoughts
don't come in perfect sentences
they come in buckets
of movement and emotions
all mixed in with the occasional
words

how strange
how liberating
to not fill the entire space with
words

allowing us so much more
space
to
roam
about

breathing
and interweaving
with the words
as I *dance* my fingers
on these keys

* * *

the *love* fills the spaces
the *magic* fills the silences

the stanzas are filled with
just these words
to connect you to me

* * *

all I crave is this *touch*
linked through these words
and the *wide spaces*
in-between

The Womb of Gentleness

you said
I don't feel safe.
what's happening to me?

so I gently plucked you from
the milky way
and placed you back in my womb

the *darkness* is temporary
my love
the *white noise* lulls you to go
deeper within

take in
my *love*
my *pride*
my *joy*

let me gently rock you to safety

* * *

rest, my child
grow well, my child
stretch, my child
be strong, my child

you deserve all the time you need

to be
rebirthed
again

My Journey

How I navigate through life using the lens of Gentleness.

A Sweet Bee 12 Hours From Me

This poem was written for my friend Melissa Blanchard, aka Melissa Bee. :)

* * *

I've never met such a gentle, sweet bee
buzzing from the other side of the world to me

she's
kind
sweet
smart
empathetic
brave
and so great at *multitasking!*

she moves me
with her gentle encouragement

so glad that I've got one extra sun
shining 12 hours away from me

Thank you, my gentle
sweet buzzing bee
you've got a friend in me!

How Gentle Can Gentleness Be?

when I think about not thinking
my mind gets obsessed with thoughts

my emotions can go haywire
as they tear me away from my body

* * *

but *gentleness*
ah!
what a beautiful word!

so soft
so tactile
so light
so loving

beautiful butterflies
alongside blooming bee balm
soft honey hugs
wrapped up in humans

* * *

this word-*gentleness*

touches my mind so very gently
whimsical thoughts flourish
how gentle *gentleness* can be!

I let my guard down
as I enter me into me

suddenly I have giant pores
love flows freely in and out of me!

* * *

beaming with
a sunny warmth
tiny cells freed
alive and well
whirling sweetly

I dance!
my soul dances!

I'm free
agile
brimming with joy
spilling over to the world
around me

interrupting their
dazed existence
beckoning to the awakened ones to
run towards me

* * *

so we can hold hands and giggle
like kids again
playing on Earth
just like in our heavenly dreams

come dance with me!

Inside-Out

I'm playing catch-up
with bits and pieces of me flung
inside-out
fused in the people around me

there's something in them
that bonds them to me

         * * *

somehow
we are all rearranging ourselves
to see this Oneness

where all is truly well
where we can let
each moment pass
and feel eternally
free

The Heart of Empathy

I feel
but my mind denies I feel
feelings are so inconvenient
when they don't *solve and heal*

I feel
my heart says Yes!
to be human is to feel
and link with other hearts that are
so real

I feel
oh sometimes I'm not sure what I feel
but I do feel

* * *

tangles
frenzied pinballs darting around
the uniformity of density all around
like I'm submerged in a blurry ocean
but oh yes, I do feel

I feel you
even when I'm not sure it was you
even when my mind denies that was you
touching my soul

but if I allow
so very gently
to let these feelings dance and soar
as they ping-pong through my body
and deepen my soul even more

* * *

these feelings wrap me softly
in a cocoon of warmth
where you and I are inside

crying
laughing
shouting
screaming
giggling
with safety
with love
with a sense that all is well

* * *

when I surrender my life
to the heart of
empathy

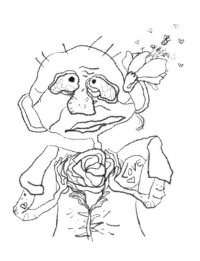

I Thank My Green Eyes

green with envy
that's what they say
when what you have
should have been mine
anyway

slimy green
thorns under roses
slippery and spiky
nauseous all over

* * *

let's pause...

and add
more peace

hot slime cools to smooth jade green
thorns start to uphold this beauty

now I see your beauty with more clarity
stepping out of my cage
running towards
dreams I finally see!

* * *

wide-eyed with sunshine blooms
my heart beams
you're my new friend
it's true!

yes!
it's crystal clear
my heart blooms with gratitude
when I truly see you

* * *

I thank my green eyes
and you

Holding Hands

I like to hold my hand
with my hand from all times
reaching out for my child self
and sometimes to a
wiser and older me

soothing my childhood pains
telling her that I see it now
those moments of intense boredom
fill me and propel me to
dance out of that
damn box

* * *

the box that
suffocated
and stifled
my childhood imagination

I run on such limited vocabulary
I still haven't allowed me to
listen more
feel more
taste more
smell more
explore more
indulge more
it shows

* * *

but now I know
more than the younger me

I'm
breathing more
being still more
laughing more
reflecting more
healing more
hugging more
kissing more
asking for more

my box expands
I dance and roam and spin around
whee!
exploring what makes me Me

* * *

my future Me
pats me lightly on my head
she's amused
why I'm trying so damn hard

I feel her
love
trust
faith
patience
soulful energy

infinitely bigger
than mine

* * *

she says
don't struggle
just be
do things that arise from your being
delight in your doing

the air around me rejoices with me!

* * *

I'm amazed by
how timeless
I AM

Car Rides

I sit at the back of my dad's car
as a little girl
watching the other cars zoom by

yearning to lock eyes with
another soul
in another car

as we race down lit streets

I wonder
is this all real?
am I destined to know them all?

those lights!
they look so familiar!

did I conjure this world?
am I part of *The Matrix*?
how much of them is in me?
and me in them?

all this busyness
while I feel so still
in my heart

there is so much magic in this world
I've yet to witness it all

My First and Only Fall

I spent my first and only fall on a road trip to Vermont
when we were living in Boston
far away from home in sunny Singapore

a wonder to behold
with our only child then
a cute toddler
hooded and snuggly
feeling tiny
in this chilling breeze
and beautiful falling leaves

* * *

but who am I kidding
I saw but didn't take it all in
as my eyes grew misty
with a heavy heart

I wasn't sure
if I could ever feel light enough
to embrace this rare vacation

when someone close to me
far away in Singapore
had fallen into an eternal sleep

* * *

I don't remember what I saw
but I felt this one and only fall
so deeply

I Build Resilience With Gentleness

I long for stability
and the confidence to declare
this is how I best serve
now and forevermore

yet
my foundation *wobbles*
my beliefs are *shaken*
am I worthless?
am I useless?
am I truly happy here in this vocation?

* * *

I leap to another stable platform
I think I can do well here
this industry is reputable
my contribution is explainable
and applaudable in the hospitals
with these patients

but I *shake*

I *shake* uncontrollably with
tears and fears
I feel too much
sobbing as I connect with all their
pains and suffering

* * *

I can't inhale
I have to let go
exhale so I can take another breath
even when there's nowhere I can go

I turn to this crumbling core within me
and try to nurse it back to a healthy glow

* * *

slowly as I grow new lives within me
being a mother exaggerates my Harshness
I try to upgrade with an
enhanced Gentleness

listening more deeply
loving more fiercely
knowing that I'm worthy

the lighter I become
the softer I melt

I start to find containers
firming up my essence
touching lives with
playfulness and lightness

believing and trusting
all is well

* * *

I no longer blame myself
for leaping and crumbling
I don't need to push
to display my resilience

I was merely being water
the gentle resilience of water
strong enough to be molded
soft enough to flow away
when I'm no longer needed
resilient enough to be sculpted into
greatness

* * *

this is how I build
resilience with gentleness

I Came From The Stars

someone told me
I came from the stars
on a planet called Hadar

we'd shine a beam
of unconditional love
to help younger planets thrive

* * *

but alas
we got invaded
trampled upon
some *enslaved*
others *escaped*
our beautiful planet
gone forevermore
destroyed by forces of greed
when they were really
thirsting for

true love that *sings*

* * *

I fled to earth
with a shell for protection
for love is so dense here
and filled with transactions

for many lifetimes
I've been here
tolerating its density
familiar yet still feeling
like a newbie

* * *

this love I know
was rekindled
through pregnancies
in the form of
my three precious 'J's
and the 'M' I married

the time has come
for us to leave our home
our humble flat
for the past 11 years
where we wed
and had kids

why do I still feel heavy with grief
when I'm still on the same planet
even the same tiny country
where I've always been?

My Kitchen Heaves a Sigh of Relief

my kitchen heaves a sigh of relief
as we pack our belongings
but I can't take away
these smooth chocolate floor tiles

tethering myself to these yummy tiles
like a helium-filled balloon
needing to leave
yet still anchored
unwilling to *move*

* * *

these tiles
anchor me with these 11 years
being nurtured in this cozy home

if I leave
when I leave
will these memories start to fade at
a ferocious speed?

* * *

in this
pregnant pause...

filled with
gratitude
grief
loss
confusion
excitement
childlike wonder

a flurry of motion

packing up
holding
releasing
clearing
storing

* * *

all the while
thanking this place
we've called our home for
more than a decade

thank you!
thank you!
thank you!

may you be free
to *bless*
another family

Sketching Buses

serving this *sheltered sentence*
my mind is filled with buses
as I have doomed myself
to sketching these vehicles

I scribble on demand
just to earn more delightful giggles
hoping with all my might
to erase those dreaded tempers

* * *

my two-year-old tyrant
runs his life on buses
he denies proper food
unless I turn it into double-deckers!

a lil' looney
getting moonier
being stuck with you
eager to wheel off from you

* * *

grateful to spend these
weird
zany
crappy
quarantine times
with you
I adore you!

Three Little Kittens

three little kittens
with or without their mittens
naughty or nice
they're just being kittens!

why should mama cat
what?! and guilt them
into being good cats?

* * *

their drama mama
needs to chill
all is well
is all they need to hear

let their mistakes be
let them find and clean their mittens
without your shrillness
your highness!

it's tiring enough
following them on their journey

give yourself a little kindness
before you become lonely

pray in the day
while they play with clay
help right their wrongs
but you don't have to go cray-cray

* * *

bless your heart
catty mom friend
hold the *peace* and *stillness*
while they claw through
with no clear plans!

let our hearts expand
to hold them and us in a
neverending magical land

I'm a Hugger Mom

I'm a serial hugger
my kids are muggers
they stole my heart
a million times over

I rarely hold another human
but I'll hang onto my family
till the minutes spillover

my loved ones are great *space-holders!*

* * *

hugging isn't always pretty
sometimes I try to hug away
tantrums and disasters
refusing to face the music
trying to bury the *inconvenient truths*

I'm a hugger
what else can I do?

I try to hug away their problems
and mine too

* * *

but...

we need to hug
what hurts
so it'll shine with
grace and truth

let's hug the warm and loving truth

Everything is Fine

everything is fine!
just beam your smile!
drink and be merry!
skip and be jolly!

slam the door on your ghosts
blink away shadows that cling
skip but avoid the potholes
it's awkward
but that's how life goes

living life in 2-D
desperately trying to stay
on the upside
denying
blinding yourself
to what's beneath

let me in
breathe more life into me
let the tears stay wet
for I've got more inside of me

* * *

I open my eyes wider
and the world is not what it seems
so much *ugliness*
pounding right onto me

as it pours rain where I live
I cry for the fires raging
where I can't see
I try my best to live
yet wonder how unfair life can be

am I worthy of this air I'm breathing?
is it okay to take up the space I use?
can I still smile and crack jokes?
as others struggle just to be?

* * *

I take it all in
letting life mix around me

I'm a *creator*
I'm a *writer*

I stir in my love
then wait and see

* * *

all is well
this I believe

Will I Break?

will I break?
I feel so weak and meek
is this world too harsh for me to take?

only if you hold on too tightly, my dear

let go
let go
let go

you won't break
if you keep falling

back

to

me

Love,
Your Higher Self

Before The Twig Snaps

traffic honks
winds howl
sheets of heavy rain hit the streets

an orange yells on TV
miracles that make me
hold my breath...

* * *

so I hold my breath
and sink beneath the rocky waves

down
down
down
deep within the ocean

letting bubbles of tension float up and
pop
pop
pop!

I sit cross-legged
feeling the safety of the soft ocean floor

befriending weird sea creatures
ancient ancestors
guiding me to safety and wonder

* * *

before
the
twig
snaps

I Empower My Life
With Gentleness

gentleness is not
a weakness
it is a beautiful
strength

it keeps me stronger
with every heartbreak
or failure

I feel more graceful
as I dissolve all internal conflicts
emerging more integrated
feeling blessed and uplifted

there's no place for harshness
as I slip further
into myself

I flow seamlessly into my life
as I go along for the ride

* * *

observing
trusting
delighting
playing
experimenting
with curiosity
co-creating
knowing that I do have a say
in all that emerges each and every day

I
empower
my life
with Gentleness

Heal Humanity

What unites us as gentle beings?

If Life Is Just a Grand Illusion

what if life is just an illusion
we can't escape?
would you mope and whine
struggle in dismay?

I'd enjoy this show with some popcorn
feel through the ups and downs
with peace in my heart

choosing to be happy requires trust
softening and opening
diving deep into this ocean of love

happiness starts with your heart
your eyes
then your lips

* * *

setting aside the troubles of each day
the pains of your life

letting a cooling breeze blow right
into the steady rhythm that beats

to transform whatever remains
into a yummy sweet dessert
to share with other hearts that fuel your warm love

to make light of one's life
reflecting upon it with an easy gaze

I guess that is my recipe to be happy
in this strange land we live in

Were You Called Down to Earth?

do you remember
you weren't always here on earth?
we were tethered so tightly to Source
bundled in bliss

but we chose to heed this call
to realize our union through separation
as we stumbled down to earth

* * *

remember
life wasn't always *this dense*
this confusing
this chaotic
this polarized

remember where you came from
so you can help from a better space
with more *kindness and gentleness*

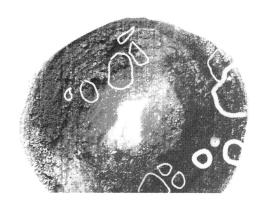

remember this gentleness

Come Home to You

sometimes it takes courage to
melt back into yourself

to feel the worry that is brewing
the anger that is simmering
the fear that is starting to
sink deeper into you

but you don't have
to be afraid

go back home to your body
face these guests
overextending their stay in you

perhaps they just need to be acknowledged
for you to lend a listening ear to

be friendly
be soft
be gentle
observe

these energies are not you
as you softly witness
they start to realize why they're here too

* * *

it is for the peace you radiate
by being here in your body

it is for the love you radiate
by staying connected to all there is

it is for you to be you
to learn from all that you feel
and emerge
being more you

* * *

you don't have
to be afraid

just come home to you

Feel

you don't have to feel the whole world
the map is right there in your body

don't weigh yourself down with
that quicksand of dramas
be the breeze seeing
what's caught *deep beneath*

feel that lump in your throat
sweaty pearls
belly butterflies
fiery anger bursting through

feel the nitty-gritty bits
breathing through the different textures
dark alleys that no one dares venture

* * *

feelings can be
intimidating
seductive
caught up in a blur

it'll be a pity not to taste them
for they form *your loving truth*

Quick Reminders

Here are some quick reminders that radiate gentleness.

Stop Moving

stop moving
around in your mind

move with
your breath
and
be still
in your mind

Slow Down

it is alright to slow down and rest
it is alright even when you feel less

just take time to be with yourself and confess
what made you feel less and feel you can't rest

Trust

trust that you'll be hurt
because life strengthens you

trust that you'll be loved
because that's who you are

trust that you will keep facing life as who you are
and love will always triumph that hurt

trust that your life is always worth
your smiles :)

Cry

crying is a sign of homeostasis
not to show how weak someone is

hold that thought
when tears fall

Ocean's Wisdom

you don't have to leap across the ocean, my dear
just admire its vastness.

Love,
From Me to me

Rebirth

Now that you are nearing the end of this book, I am celebrating your rebirth out into the light.

May you feel much safer to stay bright in our beautiful
world again.

I Used to Waffle

I used to waffle a lot
zigzagging between yes and
"erm, maybe, no I can't?"

* * *

sometimes we feel the world in us
that world isn't really
what I want

it spins
and I drag my feet
trying to hang on

* * *

then I learned to drive
time to catch up!

my huge butt zooms across highways
yes or no
I just need to show

now I get to see

the streets I'm forming
tribes I'm gathering
where the sun keeps moving
across time zones

* * *

my kids show me
No! Wins the show!
Yes! To joy like no tomorrow!

I honor
my internal *Yes, No*
my living room dances
are now proudly shown!

* * *

when in doubt
I grow still to be sure

but now
our world is unsure where to go
she keeps waffling
screaming like a toddler
her brain and heart
crumbling and re-forming

* * *

too many kids
kicking away
empires that are no longer

fun to play

it's time to recreate!

* * *

my world waits
for my *Yes* and *No*
I need to lead and run the show

I pull out my dusty pillow
running my fingers across embroidered dreams
perhaps my world wants to see them *glow*!

My Background Hum

I have a background hum
a blankie from my *Holy Mom*
after tumbling down to *earth Mom*

it's warm and soothing
a thin layer of consciousness,
where stuff unfolds with gracious aliveness

when I forget about my blankie
anger feels much more jarring
grief grips me hard and leaves me choking

* * *

I start to wonder why I'm here
in this strange coldness

but when I feel and hear my hum
a smile activates
keeping me nice and warm!

anger and grief look more exquisite
served on a silver plate

adding beauty to my life with
soupy compassion

* * *

my hum adds magical snowflakes to the mundane
bringing me to other souls *alive with holy hum!*

Stay Bright

stay bright
don't dim your light
you don't have to feel safe only when you hide

your smile delights
bundling warm hearts together
like a bonfire camp
we sing songs of fun and laughter

light attracts more light
and brings out more light!

* * *

light can comfort
as well as darkness

open your heart
you'll see amazing gifts in others

hang out in the brightest places
where angels in humans and heaven soar high

More about Bingz and Yuanhui

Thank you so much for reading this book!
Here are some quick introductions about us
*~**Bingz Huang** (author) and **Yuanhui Chen** (illustrator).*

About the Author

Bingz Huang is a proud mom of three young sons, an inspirational storyteller, an intuitive healer, and a Gentleness Coach. She is a certified practitioner in The Wonder Method, The Aroma Freedom Techniques, and is a Level 1 Human Design Specialist. Her academic education in Mechanical Engineering and Physiotherapy has nurtured her love for continually learning and experimenting with various modalities for healing.

As she stumbled through life, trying to discover her true calling and to feel safe and free being herself, she realized that Gentleness is the magical ingredient to empower her own life and others. She freed herself from the harshness of trying to fulfill this imaginary spiritual obligation to fulfill a fixed life purpose. Life is more about feeling safe to continually daydream and follow your heart's desires, while learning to give and receive in every relationship.

She has since written and published a book titled: *Empower Your Life with Gentleness: A Simple Guide to Feeling Safe and Free to be You*, interviewed 11 Gentleness Ambassadors from all walks of life, and started a new online publication,

Gentleness Ambassadors, where sensitive writers on Medium.com are gathered together to contribute their thoughts and insights on Gentleness.

Using her unique blend of training in Human Design and intuitive healing skills, she helps fellow sensitive souls understand and manage their sensitivity more effectively, so they can feel more empowered to shine their light.

Bingz invites you to connect with her through these links:
www.bingzhuanghealer.com
bingzhuang.medium.com
medium.com/gentleness-ambassadors

About the Illustrator

Yuanhui Chen (Shimmer) is a children's book illustrator, former seasoned arts educator, education analyst, and the mother of a beautiful little girl, Miss S.

She runs a learning and growing space for children authors, "Stories By Children", with the belief that children can contribute to a better world through their authentic voices. Besides running the center, she enjoys quality time with Miss S, drawing, playing, dramatizing, making art, and being silly.

An avid creator of children's literature, Yuanhui writes and illustrates children's books at Shimmer Shineworks. In her free time, she also contributes to the community as an art healer.

Holding a Master of Education (Arts in Education) from Harvard University and with her 16 years of experience in the education industry, Yuanhui dreams of *healing the world, one children's story at a time*.

Yuanhui invites you to connect with her through these links:

www.storiesbychildren.love
www.shimmershineworks.com